Late Night Talk Show Fantasy & Other Poems

JEN "PEN" —
CONGRATULATIONS ON
WINNING THE BOOK LAUNCH
LATE NIGHT TRIVIA QUIZ!
#1ST PLACE — THAT'S GREAT
BRAGGING RIGHTS!
THANKS FOR YOUR
ENTHUSIASTIC SUPPORT!
BEST VERSES,

Late Night Talk Show Fantasy & Other Poems

By

Jennifer Dotson

Cover design by Shay Culligan

Cover art by Cheryl Steiger

ISBN: 978-1-952326-03-5

Kelsay Books
502 South 1040 East, A-119
American Fork, Utah 84003

This collection is dedicated to David Dotson, my husband

Acknowledgments

Grateful acknowledgment is made to the editors of the publications in which these poems first appeared, sometimes in slightly different versions or with different titles:

Print & Online Literary Journals

After Hours: "Apology to My Books," "Beer, an Etheree"

Caravel Literary Arts: "Pathogen Rampage"

Dupage Valley Review: "Aunt Helen's Farm," "Dad's Saturday Secret," "Cooking Together"

East On Central: "Alzheimer's Disease," "Armchair Explorer's Villanelle," "Demeter Mourns," "Driving Lessons," "Edwin Booth's Dagger," "Late Night Talk Show Fantasy," "Living with a Beanstalk Boy," "Moose," "Poetry Rain," "Summer Heat," "The Secret Life of Three," "Tiny House Poem"

Exact Change Only: "Safety Conscious"

Highland Park Poetry's Muses' Gallery: "Bill the Bard," "Bond Age," "Dear Future Self at Age 99," "Dulce de Leche," "Images From Our Hike," "Turning Fifty"

Journal of Modern Poetry: "Advertising Cento," "Branded," "Going to the Pro-Choice March on Washington in 1989," "Space Tacos," "Time Traveler's Pantoum"

The MacGuffin: "Basic Black"

Willow Review: an excerpt from "10 Things I Learned from My Mother"

Anthologies

"Forecast" and "Passing the Crown" appear in *Distilled Lives, Volume 2,* a poetry anthology of the Illinois State Poetry Society

"I will run the North Shore Half Marathon in June" appears in *Voices & Visions of Sister Cities,* an anthology published by the Highland Park Sister Cities Foundation

"Staffs" appeared in *Art Gets In Your Eyes: Poets Respond to Highland Park's Public Art,* and "Empty Nest" appeared in *2018 Poetry Challenge: Electricity / Monsters / Golden Shovel,* anthologies published by Highland Park Poetry

Contents

III. The First Guest

IV. Wacky Non-Sequitur Comedian

I.

The Opening Monologue

Late Night Talk Show Fantasy

The world famous poet
chuckles with the late night
talk show host and the two
trade dazzling word play
for the cameras and the
studio audience while

the world famous poet
regales them with her
wacky escapades of
readings at open-mics
in European capital cities
and college campuses
across America on a
never ending tour
promoting her latest
full length book of poetry
that has been translated
into seven languages and
is featured in a film
starring Meryl Streep.

The world famous poet
keeps to herself that it is
neither the paparazzi
nor the inability to enjoy
a restaurant meal without
someone suggesting
what would make a
really great poem that
causes her to tremble and
twitch; it's the anxiety

that the words will stop
coming at all. Still
the world famous poet
drinks the champagne
and rides the bubbles
of public admiration
for her honest, accessible
verse and for making
poetry popular again
while not alienating
the academic crowd.

Demeter Mourns

Rage
I am consumed
My blood is flame
My screams will
shake the temple
stones to dust
She is gone
stolen away
My daughter
My baby
Taken by force
Taken by deceit
and Darkness
She would never
willingly abandon
her mother so I
rage
My grief and loss
becoming molten
scorching the earth
shriveling the harvest
turning all the green
and growing things
to grit and sand
that scrapes the skin
Ice and snow will
mass and move
and crust the land
No peace no grace
no mercy for those
that remain until
she be returned to me

The Secret Life of Three

Jesus, Mary and Joseph
the most famous family
but do we really know them?
What the Bible doesn't discuss
are Jesus' teen years.

Hidden behind closed doors
and shuttered windows
  they argue.
They argue about
  Joseph's struggling carpentry business.
They argue about
  the texture of Mary's hummus.
They argue about
  how long Jesus takes in the shower.
Their voices low
they hiss and snarl
they spit and snap
so the neighbors won't
hear the bitter exchange.

The next day
the masks slip on
the beatific smiles
and halos firmly in place.

Living with a Beanstalk Boy

Teenage boy knows everything
so he takes our only cow to sell
at the market and returns with
some magic beans and shrugs
whatever when I yell and scream
and choke on tears and bitterness.
I am back to my endless chores
of dishes and laundry, pausing only
to stare hungrily at the empty
pantry and wonder when the
power and the phone will be
turned off for good.

He may have found a goose
laying golden eggs but now
there's a dead giant in our
backyard and the neighbors
complaining of the smell.
The village forester insists
the enormous vine growing
on our property could be an
invasive species because it's
not native and he's issuing
a citation for planting without
a permit.

I wish I had my cow back—
loyal and dependable with
warm nose and docile demeanor.
Instead I'm saddled with my son,
an oaf, a fool, a typical teen
who'd rather skip school and
climb the stalk of adventure.

Bill the Bard, an Etheree[1]

Will
Shakespeare
Glover's son
Husband of Anne
Lord Chamberlain's Man
In London he did span
the Globe with his many plays
400 years since we're amazed
at his skill in illuminating
with art the motives of the human heart

---

[1] The Etheree, a syllabic poem containing ten lines and a total of fifty-five syllables, is named in honor of Etheree Taylor Armstrong, an Arkansas poet who died in 1994.

Edwin Booth's Dagger

The dagger is in a glass case
in his Grammercy Park home
now both museum and respite
for itinerant actors in New York.
If objects have auras, then this
dagger holds the ghosts of a
multitude of Hamlets, cosmic
echoes of the Master, Edwin.
His sweat, his bravado, his
very flourish are trapped for
eternity in the richly decorated
leather and paste gems that
adorn its sheath. Few remember
but he was a giant on the stage.
Both women and men gasped
upon the fire in his eyes and
the passion in his voice
carrying them to Denmark and
to Elsinore. Only after his
brother's dreadful act
screaming *Sic Semper Tyrranis*
in his egotistical madness
was Edwin covered by a
shroud of guilt for the remainder
of his days. The focus shifted
and fixed upon his status as
the brother of a monster
and not his plays.

Branded

Lindsay Wagner was my idol as
Jamie Sommers, the Bionic Woman.
I felt empowered because she was
empowered literally with her bionic
legs and bionic arm and a bionic ear
(not an eye like her lover, Steve Austin,
The Six Million Dollar Man).
She could toss a bad guy across a room,
hear incriminating conversations far
away through walls.

I played games with the doll in her
image and her secret spy laboratory
that doubled as a beauty salon.
I wrote her letters expressing my
devotion though she didn't reply.
I received a photograph with a printed
signature, no personal message and
an offer to join her official fan club
for a small fee.

Decades have gone by.
Lindsay Wagner maintains her brand
while selling Sleep Number Beds to the
generation that loved her and is now
grown older. I wear my grey hair short,
unashamed and unafraid. She
maintains the same long-haired locks
of Jamie Sommers with her frozen
smile reduced to pitching a mattress
for bad backs, a body part not enhanced
by bionics.

Advertising Cento

Have you met life today?
Where's the beef?
What's in your wallet?
Does she or doesn't she?
Maybe she's born with it,
maybe it's an
ancient Chinese secret.
A little dab'll do you.
You're in good hands.
You're soaking in it.
You deserve a break today.
Just do it.
You can do it, we can help.
So easy a caveman can do it.
Be all that you can be.
Sometimes you feel like a nut,
sometimes you don't.
Life tastes good.
Snap! Crackle! Pop!
Finger lickin' good.
Good to the last drop.
Obey your thirst.
Taste the rainbow.
Eat fresh!
It melts in your mouth
not in your hands.
Two great tastes that
taste great together.
Breakfast of champions.
They're magically delicious.
Oh what a feeling!
Oh what a relief it is.
It's the real thing.
Have it your way.
Take me away to the

Happiest place on Earth.
I'd walk a mile for
taking care of business
when it absolutely positively
has to be there overnight.
When there is no tomorrow.
Head for the border.
Head for the mountains.
Fly the friendly skies.
Put a tiger in your tank.
Unleash the jaguar.
Unleash the beast.
Zoom zoom zoom!
The City never sleeps,
The best never rest.
Like a good neighbor,
a diamond is forever.
It keeps going and going and going.
Between love and madness
lies obsession.
Let your fingers do the walking.
Reach out and touch someone.
I'm loving it.
Double your pleasure,
double your fun.
Let's build something together.
Priceless.

Sources: 1 Metlife, 2 Wendy's, 3 Capital One , 4 Clairol, 5-6 Maybelline, 7 Calgon Detergent, 8 Brylcream, 9 Allstate Insurance, 10 Palmolive, 11 Kit Kat, 12 Nike, 13 The Home Depot, 14 Geico Insurance, 15 U.S. Army, 16 Mounds & Almond Joy, 18 Coca-Cola, 19 Rice Krispies, 20 Kentucky Fried Chicken, 21 Maxwell House Coffee, 22 Sprite, 23 Skittles, 24 Subway, 25 M&Ms, 27 Reese's Peanut Butter Cups, 29 Wheaties, 30 Lucky Charms, 31 Toyota, 32 Alka-Seltzer, 33 Coca-Cola, 34 Burger King, 35 Calgon 36 Disneyland Park, 37 Camel Cigarettes, 38 The Office Depot, 39 FedEx, 42 Taco Bell, 43 Busch Beer, 44 United Airlines, 45 Esso, 46 Jaguar, 47 Monster Energy Drink, 48 Mazda, 49 Citibank, 50 Ford, 51 State Farm Insurance, 52 De Beers Consolidated Mines, Ltd., 53 Energizer Batteries, 54 Calvin Klein's Obsession, 56 Yellow Pages, 57 AT&T, 58 McDonald's, 59 Wrigley's Doublemint Gum, 61 Lowe's, 62 Mastercard

Space Tacos

The challenge of tacos
in zero gravity of outer
space is that there is no
gravity to hold things
in place and keep them
together.

On the shuttle or space
station, variety of menu
is appreciated. MRE's
lack flavor and astronauts
hunger for home to keep it
together.

I want tacos and have my
NASA-version of refried
beans, meat, cheese and
salsa but the tortilla floats
away while I put them
together.

I dance with my tortilla
and spread beans as my
sticky base to anchor
other items. Our pas-de-
deux complete when folded
together.

The result is better than
expected. On Earth these
wouldn't rate on any foodie's
plate but here my mouth and
memory relish the effort
together.

The Election, a Gwawdodyn[2]

It's time again for deep reflection
about our candidate's direction.
Tension mounts at polls because each vote counts.
Mark your ballot with your selection.

Smear campaigns are a foul infection,
swaying minds for party defection.
Strident voices make confused our choices;
civil candidates fear rejection.

Past actions demand our inspection.
Change of heart causes course correction.
Don't do it by rote; think about your vote!
We hope for change—future perfection!

---

[2] Gwawdodyn is a Welsh poetic form comprised of quatrains with a 9/9/10/9 syllable pattern and matching end rhymes on lines 1, 2 and 4. The third line contains an internal rhyme.

How to Prepare for Disaster

The end of the world is near
and you are getting ready
just in case the Mayan calendar
is accurate after all and
Nostradamus knew a thing
or two about Arab Spring. You
are getting ready for World War III
and the Asian flu pandemic that
spawns the zombies and attracts
the aliens and the electromagnetic
pulse from solar flares that turns off
all the power and the big earthquake
that knocks California off the map.
You are prepping for when the
giant asteroid hits and Yellowstone's
caldera of molten magma erupts and
blankets us in volcanic ash and
tornados, hurricanes and tsunamis
take out all the rest and you are
stockpiling supplies and readying
your go bag. Just remember
that there is more to survival
than the rule of three
that says you can survive
three minutes without air and
three days without water and
three weeks without food because
what will you pack for your
mental survival? How will you
keep your wits as you hunker
down in your bunker and calculate
the slow passage of time until
the radiation levels are safe
for you to forage for more supplies?
Will you rely on rapidly melting

memories while you ration out the
MREs and bottled water?
Make sure you have some
reading matter along with
your matches and duct tape,
your can opener and your candles.
Your eyes will quickly glaze
over tomes on growing that garden
or catching some squirrels for stew.
Be sure to add a great book or
two to read aloud by candle flame
like *Great Expectations* or *Treasure
Island* or some modern master
of fiction to transport you far
away from thoughts of panic
and what's the point of staying
alive if you have to eat roaches
to thrive in the days after disaster.
Since I am a poet and this is a poem,
I urge you to have some poetry with you.
Maybe just a slender volume inside the
Breast pocket of your Gore-tex jacket
or a large anthology that can double
duty as a pillow to keep some beauty
within reach so you can finally puzzle
out some meaning behind the struggle
for existence when the apocalypse arrives.

Pathogen Rampage

The television doesn't work anymore
but the news anchor's stricken face
lingers in our mind as she announced
the station's final broadcast because
the pandemic was destroying
everything and everyone.

The first days as the disease touched
down on U.S. soil with the return of
weary health workers from the shores
of Death the future was still before us.
Then mobs shouted *Quarantine* and
Containment. The government set up
shelters and field hospitals which were
quickly consumed as the streets filled
with bodies and blood spreading
infection. Scientists couldn't discover
a cure for the pathogen rampage.

Now we wait holding hands in the
shadows. I wish for the sudden certainty
and quick end that Pompeii's people
knew. We could be that couple
buried in smoke and ash. Our bodies'
intimate embrace creating a void
for future archeologists to make
plaster molds inspiring others with
our passion in spite of impending Death.
But the fever is in our bloodstream
carving out voids in our insides, in our
DNA and our skin is become paper thin
that too much touch is too hard to bear.

Just the press of hot palms and
fingers as we shake and shiver
parched and waiting for oblivion.
We do not wish to be alone when
the End arrives.

II.

The House Band

Dulce de Leche

My stepfather lived for a time
in Majorca and told us about
dulce de leche and
how the women slowly stirred
the sweet milk in a double boiler
in endless circles until the magic
transformation from pale cream
to a caramel-hued miracle.
He dreamed of recreating this in
our Brooklyn apartment but without
the endless hovering and stirring.
He put a large pot of water on the
stove over a low flame and lowered
in a can of sweetened condensed milk
and let it boil for four hours.
We'd hear it bump against the sides
of the pot. My mother was afraid the can
would burst in angry lava but the eruption
never happened. Lured by danger, we'd
check the can's movement.
Four hours seemed forever.
Finally declared done, he opened it and
we dipped in delicate spoons savoring
the sweet warmth on our tongues.

Aunt Helen's Farm

Aunt Helen's house perches
high on the hill that slopes
down to the pond, Turtle Cove,
and the road beyond.
In summer we swim its
brown-green water, fearful of
snapping turtles like hungry
dinosaurs beneath the surface.
Make noise and splash a lot;
your toes will be safe she says.

In winter we rocket down
the hill our sleds flying
on crusty crunchy snow and
rough ice of the frozen pond
eager to make it all the way
across to opposite bank
and the road beyond.

One spring Uncle John's dog
nosed a black plastic garbage bag
from among the pond's reeds.
Edges ragged from a turtle's
curiosity, shrouding a newborn
someone tossed while driving
on the road beyond.

Moose

Black and white mutt
with ears that perked
up like quotation marks
and a tilt of your head
to words with a hard "kuh".
Park
Quick
Squirrel
Walk
Those magic words would
launch you into a frenzied
dance of circular tail chasing
joy by the front door ready for
the metal jingle of your leash.
We could never teach you
any tricks or words with
dominant "s" sounds like
Sit or *Stay.*
Even spelling P-A-R-K didn't
keep you in the dark for long.
Your disappearance on moving
day was a deep loss.
Slipping out in between
the parade of boxes to
the truck you were gone
before you could ever
sniff out your new home.
No amount of searching
or flyers beseeching
Lost Dog ever found you.
We hoped you were rescued
by other loving humans
to adore your quirks and
unique character.
Closure came years later

when the Parisian psychic
swore she sensed your
unmistakable presence
in the photograph of
Mom, Izzy and me
with Statue of Liberty
welcoming the world
above our heads.
We knew then you
remained loyal to
our crew, your
unconditional love still
keen to guard and protect.

Dad's Saturday Secret

Restaurants were a treat
but as a child you quickly learn
your choices are limited
to the narrow offerings
on the kids menu
So imagine the thrill
on a Saturday visit
when Dad smiles and says
Order whatever you want.
My choice was the Deluxe
Cheeseburger platter
with coleslaw, French fries
and a giant pickle spear.
Dad smiles at the waitress,
I'll have a plain liverwurst sandwich.
The food arrives looking
just like the glorious photo
on fulfilling the promise
of the laminated menu.
We tuck in to our meals.
I am quickly overwhelmed
by the volume of food before me.
My appetite filled and the
capacity of my stomach
significantly smaller than
my wishes. Dad smiles again
and polishes off the remainder.

This successful strategy
served him well years later
with subsequent siblings
who recount similar
experiences at Denny's.
Order what you like.
Dad selects a simple

garden salad side while the
boys choose spaghetti and
meatballs and chocolate
chip pancakes. His secret
to being a hero was
allowing us to make
extravagant choices,
giving us the power
to order whatever we
wanted, knowing he
would finish most of it.

Baby Alive is Dead

Izzy's favorite doll
was Baby Alive, a
battery-powered
monster whose latex
lips moved to mimic
drinking a bottle or
crying, *Ma Ma.* Most
magical was feeding
Baby Alive and then
changing her diapers
just like a real baby.
Baby Alive went
everywhere Izzy went.

But once the batteries
had worn out and been
removed, our mother
let Izzy take a bath
with Baby Alive.
Baby had to stay in
the tub to dry out
and soon one bath
became two baths
became three baths
and now Baby Alive
lived in our tub taking
up residence on the
narrow white tile ledge
crammed with our family's
shampoos and soaps.

Taking a shower during
Baby Alive's reign was
dangerous and creepy.
Her eyes popped open

wide and staring at you
as you shampooed and
rinsed. It was common
to hear a crash and curses
as Baby Alive dove down
to the bath mat tumbling items
into the tub with her
to the surprised alarm
and annoyance of the
person showering.

Days turned to weeks
turned to months and
finally our mother said
Enough. Baby Alive was
destined for the trash.
But before she departed
we wanted to satisfy our
curiosity about her inner
workings. Izzy agreed
to the autopsy and our
older brother was given
a razor blade to slice
through Baby Alive's
fake skin. Peeling back
the outer layer revealed
a smaller inner baby
mold of what was once
a white porous substance
now almost completely
coated in dark black
mold. Long after her
prompt burial in the
trash, the exposure of
this secret horror remained.

My Mother is a Dancer, a Ghazal [3]

She studied ballet very young feeling the dance.
Hours at the barre, plié, relevé, revealing the dance.

She advanced to toe shoes at the age of only five.
Delicate bones molded because it is appealing to dance.

At Bennington she found a preference for modern,
Thus freeing her feet and healing the dance.

Her career as a choreographer in New York was hard;
She discovered there was a glass ceiling in dance.

Age limits a body's abilities says the sage Capricorn.
Old injuries betrayed her till she was kneeling the dance.

---

[3] A Ghazal is a poetic form of Persian origin, consisting of five or more complete
couplets linked by rhyme and the repetition of a closing word or phrase.

Driving Lessons

I. Ignition

On a Sunday visit Dad suggests
Why don't you drive the Valiant?
My 12-year old feet stretch for pedals—
Gas on right, brake on left.
We switch places one block
down the street to his driveway.
Hands on the wheel at ten and two.
Pressing on the gas unleashes
a sudden surge like a chained
up dog after a squirrel. Nothing
like Dad's smooth handling behind
the wheel, the Plymouth creeps
and jerks under my command.

II. Pressure Plate

Too young to take Driver's Ed
at Springbrook High, I decline
Latin conjugations instead
ago agis agit agimus agitis agunt.
A College junior at eighteen,
I am determined to learn
on my summer break.
Sears Driving School sends
Mr. Johnson to instruct me.
Today we're going to learn drive-thru.
Not as simple as it sounds.
Pull the car close enough to the
menu microphone but not too close
to damage the mirror or door.
Mr. Johnson orders himself lunch.

I repeat the close but not too close
lesson at the windows to pay
and to retrieve his food.
Mr. Johnson has an appetite.
Our next session ups the ante.
My first time cloverleafing into
Beltway traffic, Mr. Johnson purrs
You would look fine in a pair of
black leather pants. My hands grip
the wheel, focus flits to the cars
around me, my mirrors and pressing
down on the gas. Is this a test
or calculated distraction from the
crushing rush of other drivers?
Nervous, I say nothing—not then,
not later—too afraid to lose my
chance to learn *agere*—to drive.

I have no learner's permit and am
not allowed alone in the Sear's car
with its second steering wheel
and pedals should I lose control.
Mr. Johnson says today's lesson is
to follow him as he drives his
parent's car from the mechanic's
shop to their home. He motions
me to roll down the window.
Don't fuck this up.

III. Brake

Practice session with Uncle John
in grandma's beige Chevy Impala.
I learn the most important rule of the
road—*Beware old men in hats.* They love
to go just under the speed limit but
will accelerate if you attempt to pass.
Get behind one and you're doomed.
Sometimes they disguise their identity.
Sometimes they take off their hats.

IV. Emission

Months later before my test,
my grandmother suggests a
refresher lesson from Sears.
Shall I ask for Mr. Johnson?
No, not necessary. Any instructor
will do. He is no longer employed
by Sears and the new instructor
is amazed that after all my previous
lessons I've never heard of a
three point turn nor have I
tried to parallel park.

V. Combustion/Clutch

In my early 20's I struggle
with learning to drive a stick
shift in my husband's orange
Fiat Spider convertible. His
napkin drawn diagrams
about a car's inner works
make my head swim in
thick incomprehension.
On the road I try to imitate
what I see him do naturally
but the grinding and stalling
are humiliating and worse are
his barked corrections. I retreat
from the field to my shell of tears.

VI. Independent Suspension

Necessity is the Mother of invention
or so they say but my Mother's
necessity taught me stick shift.
Flying cross-country to be with
her post-surgery, the only vehicle
available is her white Toyota
truck with manual transmission.
Ordinarily she loves driving her
trusty truck over Oregon's roads
but she can't operate it with her
abdomen stitched and bandaged.

With doctors' appointments to
get to, I am the only one available.
Failure is not an option and I find
my rhythm through trial and error.
Mother offers encouragement.
Medication numbs her pain but
she feels every jolt and stall.
We manage and I return home
with new confidence to practice
in my husband's blue Ford Fiesta
in an empty corporate parking
lot on a Sunday afternoon.

VII. Transmission

I lack patience with my teenaged
son and daughter. I prefer to let
their father or their driving
instructors live through the
white knuckle moments without
me. I wait until they have some
lessons before I get in the passenger
seat and buckle up for the ride.
Today we're going to learn drive-thru.

When My Mother Met John Travolta

During one of those fallow periods
between choreographic enterprises
when paying rent was primary,
my mother worked at Henri Bendel,
the store for New York's monied elite.
She told tales of wealthy customers
spending thousands on Egyptian
cotton sheets with a thread count
as fine as feathers floating above
the mattress or smooth designer jeans,
duvets and cashmere socks in assorted
candy color shades.
My mother would sometimes be
summoned to the eyrie of administration.
My mother rode the elevator,
a clipboard pressed against her chest
when he entered on the main level
accompanied by a personal shopping
assistant assigned just for his visit.
My mother was a New Yorker,
trained to feign nonchalance in the
presence of a celebrity.
Her expression neutral, she snuck
sideways glances to exult in being
in so small a space with someone so
famous so part of our culture's
consciousness with *Welcome Back
Kotter* and *Saturday Night Fever.*
He smiled knowing she knew who
he was, knowing his impact
and the sudden loss of oxygen
in the box. My mother watched
him exit and inhaled.

10 Things I learned from my Mother

1. There is no substitute for real butter.
2. The dough is ready when the hand mixer motor gives off that slightly burning smell.
3. The Laundry giveth and the Laundry taketh away and mostly unmatched single socks.
4. Always carry a bag large enough to rival Mary Poppin's magic carpet bag.
5. A well wrapped package requires excessive amounts of packing tape.
6. The highest scoring words in Scrabble are not always the longest; the game may be won with a single well placed letter.
7. To be considered quality dating material, a man should be able to pick you up—literally.
8. The best cold remedy ever is a hot toddy—a large mug with whiskey, lemon juice, honey and boiling water. Breathe in the steam and sip slowly.
9. You will have lots of jobs in the course of your life but they do not define you; you are more interesting than your résumé.
10. Likewise, cultivate interests other than your children —they will leave you.

Passing the Crown

Scrabble is not just a game
for our family. It is history.
It is a code of conduct for fair play.
It is a heritage of word-wise
women and men who place
their "X" on a triple word score
and vault their tally of points
far above the other players.
It is knowing how to survive
when the bag of tiles gives
you only vowels. It is a
measure of maturity to play
with the adults, anxious to
compete but absorbing the
blows of superior skills.
Yesterday, I beat my mother
after decades of losses.
She smiled, sighed and
handed me her crown.

Family Harmony Sonnet

Why do different things bother us so much?
Our son hates fruit and even just the smells
send him from a room. Or things mustn't touch
like ceramic plates on paper towels.
I can't hear it but he swears it sounds
to him like nails scraping on a chalkboard.
Stacks of books and papers are my kin's grounds
for accusations that I tend to hoard.
Since our daughter can't stand any clutter,
shoes must be ordered within her wardrobe.
My husband sees germs abound and flutter.
He hopes to fend off attack by microbe.
If in harmony we aspire to live,
we must to others quirks be sensitive.

Easy Math: a love poem

We plan our escape
when the children are
gone just two days away
or forty-eight hours and
twenty three miles from
our front door.
The digits don't matter
as we calculate the spent
moments with interest on
how to solve for X,
the delicious intangible
we hope to find hidden
behind the door of the
sleek modern hotel room
on the twenty-second floor.

We test the proof while
dividing our attention to
enjoying geometry of planes
and attractive angles created
by furnishings and floor-to-
ceiling glass windows.
To sum up we're just two
figures making Venn diagrams
and multiplying measures
of exponential pleasure
until check-out time.

Cooking Together

It wasn't my first BBQ.
When we met, I feared
I was just a crust,
a shell, a broken yolk
but your savory attention
set my broth to boil.
You whisked my batter
to a froth and I quickly
flipped my outlook on
life and love.
You didn't sear me
with your flame
leaving my insides
raw or frozen,
instead you braised
me with wine and herbs
and I've been simmering
your spicy stew ever since.

Empty Nest[4]

A Golden Shovel Poem with line from Emily Dickinson's #1540

We looked forward to becoming empty-nesters as
one by one the children left home. Imperceptibly
we're surprised at the sudden silences as
we find ourselves alone together. My unexpected grief
at adding entries with their new addresses in the
book because before our home was their home. Summer
ended dropping them off at their universities. Time lapsed
differently. We yearn to hold them now that they're away.

---

[4] A Golden Shovel is a poetic form developed by Terence Hayes to honor poet Gwendolyn Brooks. Using text from an admired poem, the words become the end words for each line in a new poem, whose content does not need to refer to the original text.

III.

The First Guest

Basic Black

Some say I've no sense of fashion.
What to wear is not my passion.
One single rule keeps me on track:
it's always stylish to wear black.

I'm lousy with accessories.
No belts or scarves, if you please.
French women are born with the knack.
C'est dramatique to dress in black.

In middle age I've grown some pudge
that diet and exercise won't budge.
My downfall is I love to snack.
It's always slimming to wear black.

In spring and summer some give voice
to criticize my color choice.
My one defense to this attack?
It's always stylish to wear black.

Turning Fifty

How nifty to
be turning fifty.
In Shakespeare's
time I'd be past
my prime and
looking grave.
Now I shift
the paradigm
and join in making
lists of mountains
to climb. Chalking
up new experiences
before my half full
bucket empties out.

Flash

I feel cold
I feel hot
I don't know
which is which
God or hormones
flip a switch
and I perspire
radiating sudden fever
not from stress
or even desire
but a thermostat
on the fritz
I toss blankets
take off clothes
still I schvitz
Then it goes
leaving me damp
until the next
episode

I will run the North Shore Half Marathon in June

Slowly patiently
Building endurance
Increasing distance
Overcoming obstacles
Plowing persistence to harvest
My dream of 13.1 miles
I run   I am a runner
My stride lengthens
My breath flows
Steadily evenly
Inhale and exhale
A metronome keeping time
Step after step becomes ¼ mile
Becomes ½ mile becomes 1 mile
And each mile is dedicated
A gift of prayer for my family
And loved ones
I carry their image with me
In my mind's eye
We converse without words
As I pass the mile markers
And the water stations
The landmarks like Ravinia
Glimpses of Lake Michigan
Gently sloping hills
That make my thighs burn
Feet dance off pavement
Past Rosewood Beach
Press forward push north
To Park Avenue Beach
Steep curving drive that knows
What goes down must go up again
Continuing past Sheridan Road manors
Until I reach the Fort
My shoulders release

I let go of the cramp
In my back or the ache
In my left knee
I radiate strength and power
A particle of energy
Hurtling through space
On my orchestrated
Orbit of Highland Park
With 5,000 other sweating
Runners urging me
On to the finish
Where the glow
Of achievement
Crowns my
Being and
I rest

Safety Conscious

I wear my helmet when I ride my bike.
It's not much protection but it's something.
A bit of compressed foam in a molded
plastic casing with adjustable straps
to cover my head, surround my skull,
my brain, the physical root of consciousness
and beingness.

I am shocked at the riders who don't.
The women not wanting to mess
up their hair. The old men believing
it's just for kids. Or the parents
who make their kids wear a helmet
but don't wear one themselves.
Or worse, the parents who don't
make their kids wear a helmet.
It's risk and odds and rolling the dice
or maybe it's denying anything bad
can happen while pedaling around
the Skokie Lagoons on the trail thick
with walkers, runners, and cyclists
all competing for their patch of pavement.
It's physics and velocity and encountering
the Unexpected.

I carry the scars on my skin,
the memory of bruises in my body.
I carry the knowledge it could have been
so much worse. The simple miscalculation,
the glance down to adjust my water bottle
and don't see the approaching curb until
it is too late and I cannot stop myself from
falling. Skin scrapes pavement.

I was lucky. This encounter ended well.
No one plans the collision.
It's why it's called an accident.
I wear my helmet.

Conversations with my Knee

I am conversing
with my knee.
At least my knee
is talking to me.
To avoid confusion
I'd better specify
it's the left (not right).
The chatter started
after I began to
run for exercise.
The conversation
is civil but I sense
that there are limits.
Certain crossroads
once crossed could
lead to language
unbecoming and
damaging to our
relationship.
I've coddled it
with ibuprofen and
ice, purchased more
expensive shoes
and socks and inserts.
I've added vitamins
for improved joint health.
My knee is not satisfied.
Nothing quiets the noise.
Still it says, *Why don't*
you take up swimming?

Images from Our Hike

Selfie on the trail, we smile
brightly blinking into the sun

Are those silver birch? we wonder
Tree trunks limbs and leaves
an almost ghostly white

Wooden bridge over marsh
weathered gray casts shadows
on our path

Burr oak bare of leaves
limbs like long arthritic hands
knobbed knuckles and bark of
darkly furrowed wrinkles

Small purple blossoms with
yellow centers—some petals
burnt by time have shrunk
to small brown fists

Blue sky and white clouds
reflected on the pond's surface
prairie grasses bend with
breezes on the shore

You are here and a red dot
marks our location on the map
But where is here?

Alzheimers' Disease

I

The early signs are
not clearly marked
like STOP or
Children at Play
Instead illness and
malfunction materialize
gradually as smoke
tendrils creep under
the door in the deep
recesses of the mind that
curl and caress a name
making the outlines hazy
and ash-smudged with
the scent of burning

II

Soon or shortly for
Time is relative like
months and mothers
fortnights and fathers
smoke coalesces into
a cloud of bees which
hum and buzz their
hypnotic chorus
interrupting synapses
blotting out the faces
filling the hallways
clogging the passages
releasing rage

III

There is no re-set button
to push, no do-over
no escaping the
mental molasses
thick and viscous that
sludges over the last
barricades of consciousness
identity and self
erasing perceptions
fragments of memories are
carried away or submerged
in the syrup flood
that coats everything
leaving you consumed with
terror and a hunger
to go home

Dear Future Self at Age 99

Do you remember
how time crept
when we were little?
The days from Christmas
to summer holidays crawled
with terrible slowness.
But now the year
leaps through the
seasons at a rapid clip.
Does time slow for you
once again as your
centennial celebration
grows near? When friends
and peers vanish from
this plane, is it hard to
keep the forward mo-
mentum of daily living?
I hope our teeth have
held out and I'm sorry
if I didn't floss enough.
I hope our memories
are still in your possession
with your wits and
that you're keeping up
the conversation with
youth—our children,
their children and so on.
May your quick and quiet
end lead to joy everlasting.

IV.

Wacky Non-Sequitur Comedian

Beer, an Etheree

Beer
Liquid
Made from mash
Of malt and hops
Yeast microbes transform
Base grains into bubbles
Zymurgy is the science
Behind brewmasters' bottle craft
Keep your head as you quaff your ale and
Pray it's not making love in a canoe

Doughnut Philosophy or Make Mine Chocolate

Doughnuts are
circles with
no centers.

Doughnut holes
are mass named
for absence.

We eat both
to fill our
inner voids.

Scott's Fruitcake

In 2017, conservationists working in Cape Adare, Antarctica discover 106-year old fruitcake from Robert Falcon Scott's Terra Nova Expedition that appeared to be in excellent condition.

Flour, butter, eggs and sugar
are the foundation of my batter.
Mix in spices, fruits and nuts—
the dark heart of my matter.

After baking in the oven,
sew me in a linen shroud.
Dose me with sherry, brandy or rum—
you choose, I'm not particular or proud.

The liquor is rich preservative,
keeping moist my inner core.
I'll be a sweet treat for Scott
and his team of men who explore.

       * * *

Have I been sleeping or long forgotten
in this house built on the ice?
Those that brought me have since passed on.
Perhaps you'll enjoy a slice?
While I'm not too credible,
I think I'm edible.

Dionysus Has a Crisis

"Tonight I drink with friends," he said
"The question is—white or red?
Everyone likes a good Chianti—
Even my auntie from Ypsilanti.
But if there's a cheese tray at the soiree
I ought to pack my chardonnay.
For toasting nothing beats Champagne
and if I slosh, it shouldn't stain.
Yet I've a taste for something with pizzazz.
Perhaps a spicy down-under shiraz.
My friends may prefer drinking mellow
like a beau soft merlot—No,
I will also want a swallow.
Bordeaux, tempranillo, or pinot?
I could play it safe and not risqué
with a California cabernet.
I've got it—something swell
My very favorite zinfandel."

The Tiny House Poem

My poem is a tiny house of
minimalist design perfection
modeled after the Japanese
masters making the most of
small spaces and few syllables.

My poem is a tiny house
with miniature kitchen where
each bite savors compact form.
Unfolding panels reveal
collapsible furnishings for
entertaining petite friends.

My poem is a tiny house.
Admire my shrinking square
footage and steps with hidden
storage leading to a loft of
my childhood dreams. Behold
the wheels tuck under the
frame to make my poem mobile
and ready for the road.

But these tiny dimensions
cannot contain my emotional
luggage and tendency to
word hoard and image clutter.
Will I wake a hapless Alice,
my head through skylight
and arms out windows?

My poem is a tiny house
that's taken root and been
rehabbed to include several
expansive additions.

The Front Porch

Porches were invented for rain.
The perfect perch for us to enjoy
an atmospheric spectacle of buckets,
cats and dogs, torrents, streams,
deluges, drizzles, mizzles, showers
and driving rain all from the
sheltered safety of our porch.
We can breathe in deeply the
fresh scent of ozone and savor
the show in the relative dry.
Porches have other uses, true.
Good places to drink your
morning tea and read the paper
or sip that cocktail after work.
But porches were invented for rain.

Love Ghazal

The naïve believe it will happen by choosing to love.
Instead we learn the pain of losing in love.

Some think relationships are meant to last forever
while they go cruising for love.

Other warriors of the heart defend themselves by
alternately abusing or refusing to love.

Cynics keep their distance
and pretend it is amusing to love.

Common wisdom says there are plenty of fish in the sea.
C'mon let's party and go boozing for love.

It is hard to open up again
after a bruising in love.

A whistling turtle observes our search for soul mates
and find it is most often confusing in love.

Poetry Rain

It's raining poetry.
Stormy skies spouting verse.
We're wet with words,
moist with metaphors,
soaked with similes.
Images clog the gutters
and downspouts.
Rhythm on the roof
of the car creates
a turbulent tempo,
a cascade of couplets,
a shower of sonnets,
and sestinas. Windshield
wipers struggle to clear
the raining rhymes.
Streets glisten in the
shiny splash of symbols
and metres of feet
dancing towards the drains.

Summer Heat, a Luc Bat[5]

Summer heat makes me sweat.
My skin shimmering wet does soak

through my shirt; it's a joke.
How do every day folk stay dry?

When the sun is set to fry
the secret is so sly and neat:

application of heat
on tastebuds does treat and turn

attention to the burn.
Eating chilies I learn is best

setting swelter to rest.
I never would have guessed they fooled.

Our brain resets to cooled.
Hot climate cuisines schooled diet.

---

[5] Luc Bat is a Vietnamese poetic form which translates to "six / eight" and refers
to the alternating lines of six and eight syllables.

Time Travelers Pantoum

Time travelers depend on clocks
and calendars to navigate their destination.
Unprotected from the journey's shocks
one must adapt to current conversation.

When compassing your desired destination—
last week, two decades or a century ago—
quickly adopt the current mode without hesitation
or your strangeness could immediately show.

A week or two becomes decades in the flow
of time for someone lost in another past.
Don't let your other-time-ness show;
listen and pick up local jargon fast.

Becoming lost in another past,
it's hard to keep your stories straight.
Listen and pick up the local jargon fast.
Study history and improve your fate.

Some find it hard to keep their stories straight
when suffering time travel's aftershocks.
Remembered history may keep your trip great.
Time travelers depend on clocks.

Earth Changes, A.R.E. Camp 1981

Sitting around the campfire
Sunfellow told us how our
Mother Earth was angry and
soon we would see her fight back
with Earth Changes. He hoped
to inspire us to transform from
early adolescents at summer camp
into an army of environmentalists
out to reduce the carbon footprint
and find the answers to combat
the Big Oil lobbyists.

Instead we ignored his words as
so much nutty crunchy nonsense
and slipped into adulthood as if
asleep, not paying attention
to the frackers and the pipelines
and the inconvenient truths and
we let the climate change deniers
take control.

Still every time the Weather
Channel reports about the
hurricanes, floods, mudslides
and earthquakes, I remember
the campfire, Sunfellow and
Earth Changes. Maybe he was
right. Maybe the Planet wants
us to wake up and we, living in
a dream, or feeling inadequate
to the challenge, have refused
to rise. Until now.

Apology to My Books

Dear beloved characters
and the authors who
created you, please
accept my apologies.
While we are together
I am yours completely.
I hold the details of
You in my mind's eye
clearly and firmly.
But close one book to
start on the next and
you shimmer—heat
vapor on the pavement.
What's your name? It's
on the tip of my tongue.

Explorer's Villanelle

I dream of distant travels in my chair,
like waking in a gorgeous French chateau.
My wild imagination takes me there.

I enjoy adventures with some flair;
A mountain climb with boulders, slick with snow—
I dream of distant travels in my chair.

My journey needs no compass, map, or care.
I don't require a purse or portmanteau;
My wild imagination takes me there.

Perhaps I'll find an orchid, large and rare
While paddling through swamps where lilies grow.
I dream of distant travels in my chair.

I'll parasail past cliffs and into the air,
Ride sailing ships that toss me to and fro;
My wild imagination takes me there.

And when I'm done, my bed waits up the stair;
I yawn, then off to slumberland, I go,
to dream of distant travels in my chair—
My wild imagination takes me there.

About the Author

Jennifer Dotson is the founder and program coordinator for www.HighlandParkPoetry.org. Her debut poetry collection, *Clever Gretel*, received the Journal of Modern Poetry First Book Award and was published by Chicago Poetry Press in 2013. Her poems have appeared in *After Hours, Caravel Literary Arts Journal, DuPage Valley Review, East on Central, Exact Change Only, Journal of Modern Poetry, Panoplyzine, Poetry Cram, Poetry Pacific,* and *Willow Review.* Her works have also appeared in numerous anthologies including *Raising Lilly Ledbetter* (Lost Horse Press), *Distilled Lives, Volumes 2 & 4* (Illinois State Poetry Society) and *A Midnight Snack* (Poetic License Press). She facilitates writing workshops for the Highland Park Public Library's Library U Program. Read more about Jennifer Dotson and her poetry at www.JenniferDotsonPoet.com.